HAL LEONARD
STUDENT PIANO LIBRARY

Popular Piano Solos
For All Piano Methods

T0071723

Table of Contents

PLAYBACK+
Speed • Pitch • Balance • Loop

To access audio, visit:
www.halleonard.com/mylibrary

Enter Code
2171-0575-9623-5051

Book: ISBN 978-0-7935-8585-4
Book/Audio: ISBN 978-1-4803-8542-9

Visit Hal Leonard Online at
www.halleonard.com

Contact Us:
Hal Leonard
7777 West Bluemound Road
Milwaukee, WI 53213
Email: info@halleonard.com

In Europe contact:
Hal Leonard Europe Limited
42 Wigmore Street
Marylebone, London, W1U 2RN
Email: info@halleonardeurope.com

In Australia contact:
Hal Leonard Australia Pty. Ltd.
4 Lentara Court
Cheltenham, Victoria, 3192 Australia
Email: info@halleonard.com.au

Bella's Lullaby

from the Summit Entertainment film TWILIGHT

Composed by Carter Burwell
Arranged by Fred Kern

Moderately (♩ = 100)

With pedal

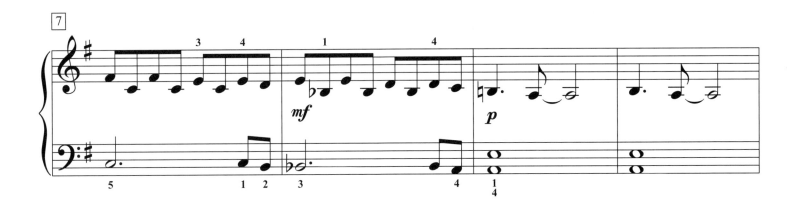

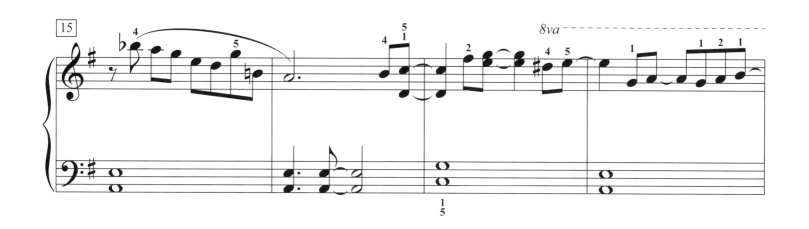

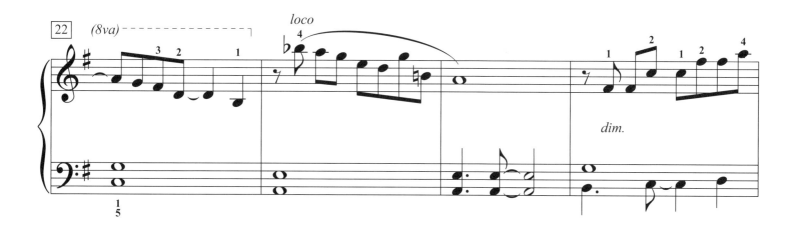

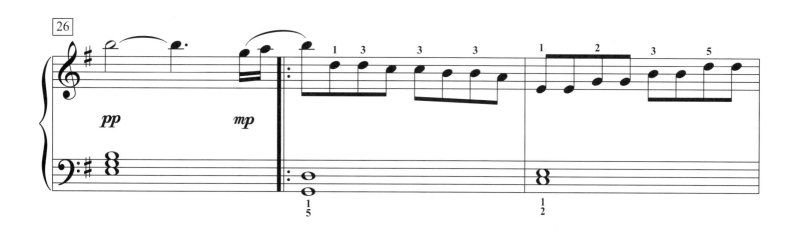

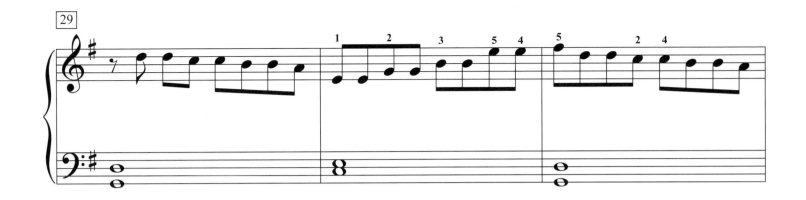

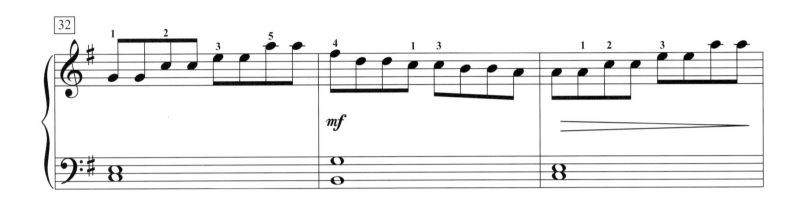

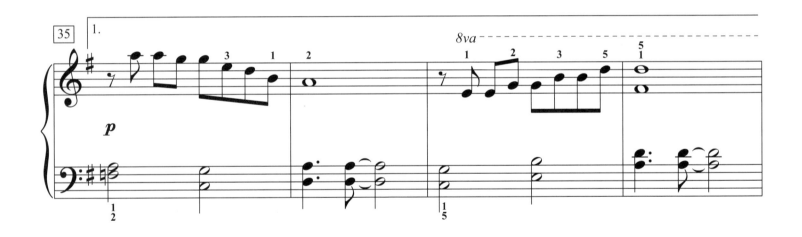

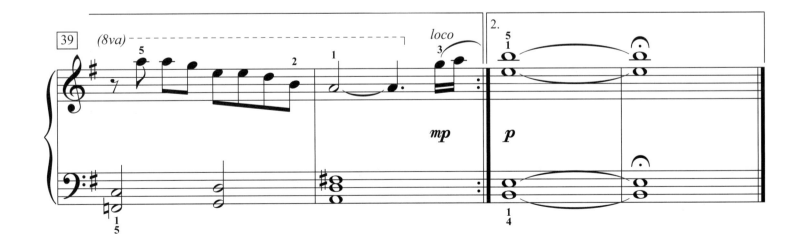

Cruella De Vil

from Walt Disney's 101 DALMATIANS

Words and Music by
Mel Leven
Arranged by Mona Rejino

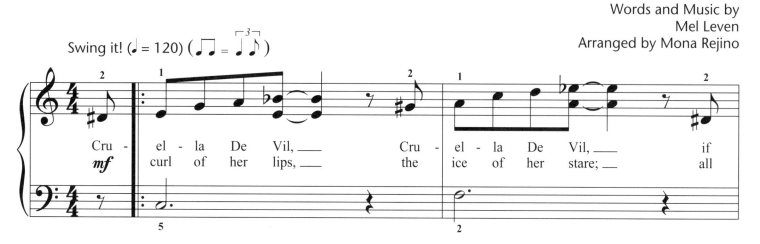

Accompaniment (Student plays one octave higher than written.)

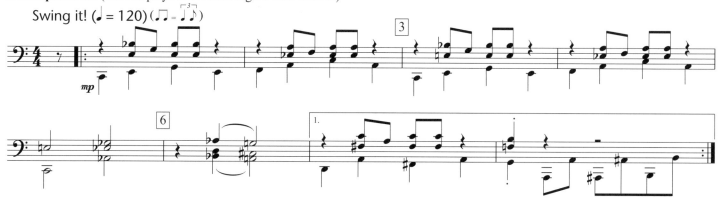

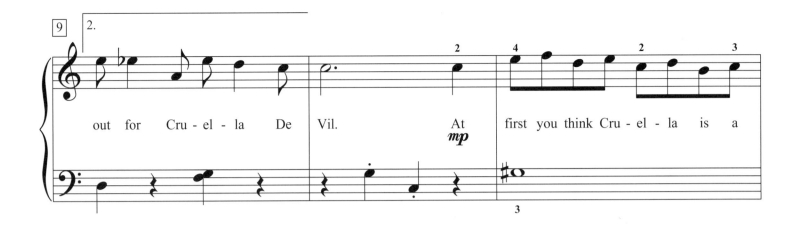

out for Cru - el - la De Vil. At

first you think Cru - el - la is a

dev - il, _____ but af - ter time has worn a - way the shock, you

come to re - a - lize you've seen her kind of eyes

watch-ing you from un - der-neath a

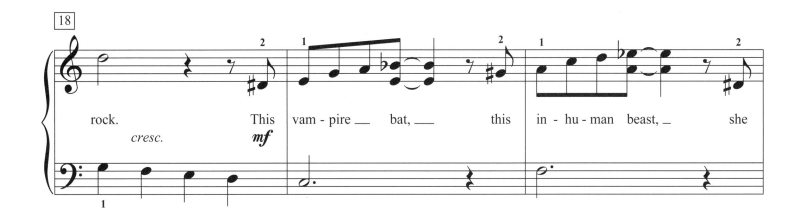

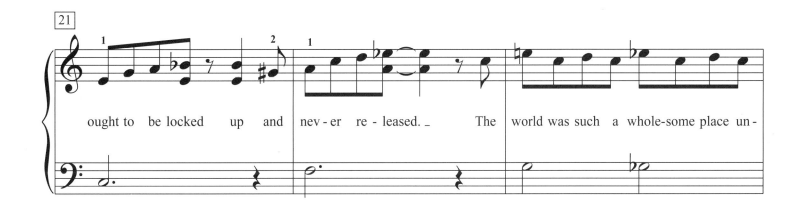

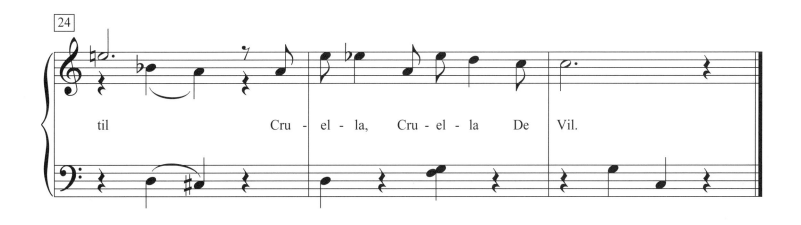

Eleanor Rigby

Words and Music by John Lennon
and Paul McCartney
Arranged by Mona Rejino

Moderately, with a steady beat (♩ = 126)

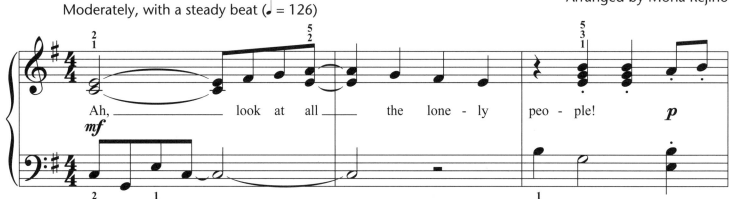

Ah, _____ look at all _____ the lone - ly peo - ple!

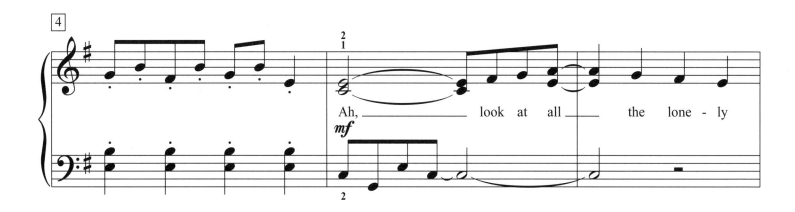

Ah, _____ look at all ____ the lone - ly

peo - ple!

El - ea - nor Rig - by
Fa - ther Mc - Ken - zie

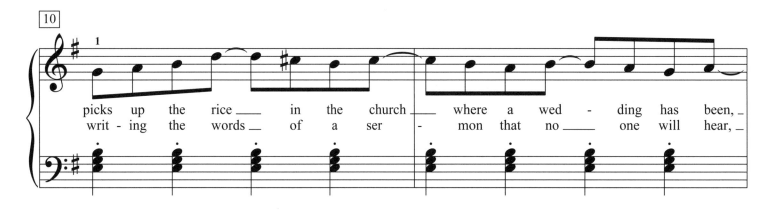

picks up the rice ____ in the church ____ where a wed - ding has been, ___
writ - ing the words ___ of a ser - mon that no ____ one will hear, ___

lives in a dream. _____ Waits at the win - dow,
no one comes near. _____ Look at him work - ing,

wear - ing the face ___ that she keeps ___ in a jar ___ by the door, _
darn - ing his socks ___ in the night ___ when there's no - bod - y there, _

who is it for? _____
what does he care? _____

mp

All the lone - ly

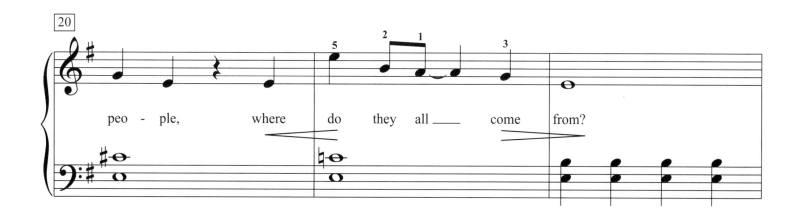

peo - ple, where do they all ___ come from?

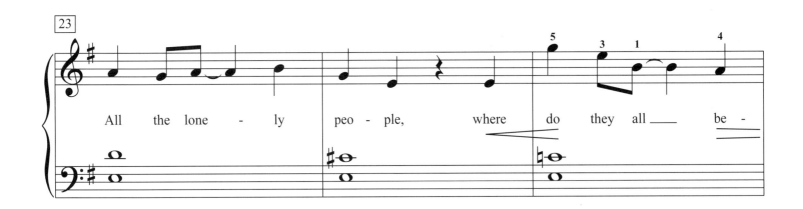

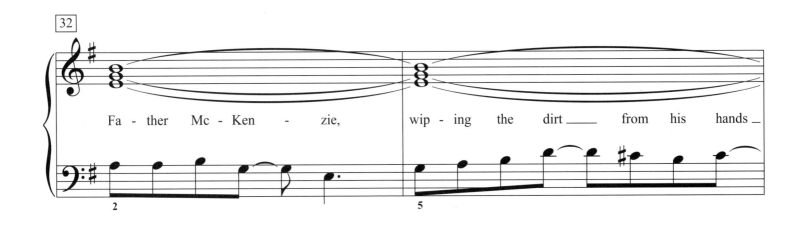

as he walks from the grave, no one was saved.

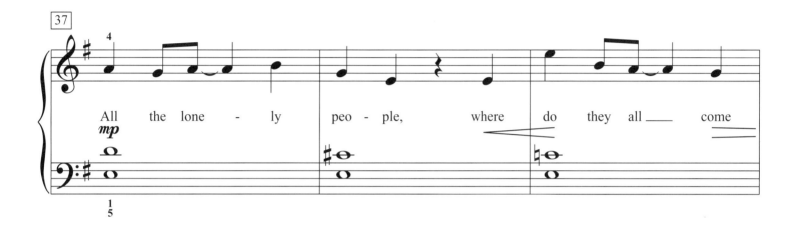

All the lone - ly peo - ple, where do they all come

mp

from? All the lone - ly peo - ple, where

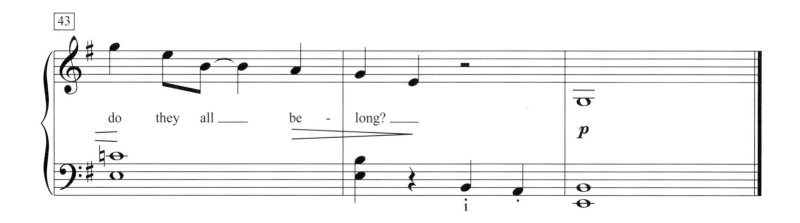

do they all be - long?

p

Hey Jude

Words and Music by John Lennon
and Paul McCartney
Arranged by Phillip Keveren

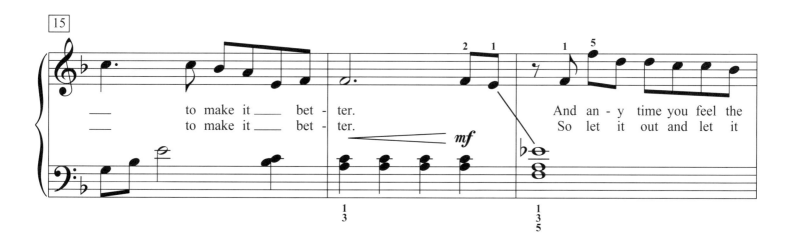

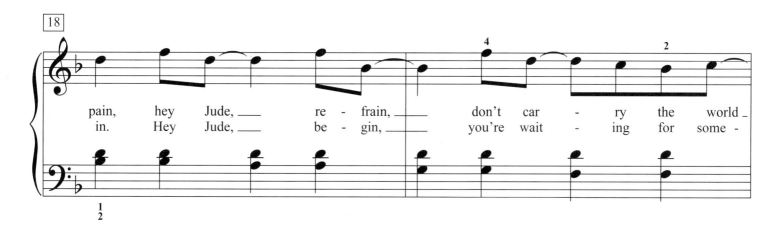

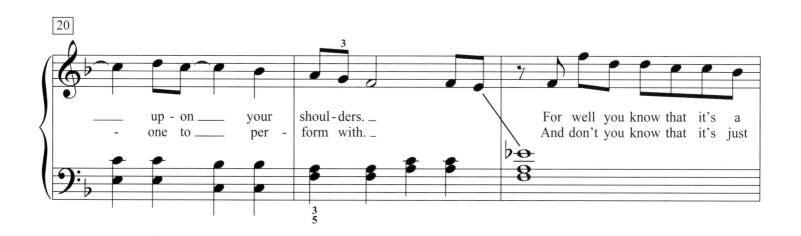

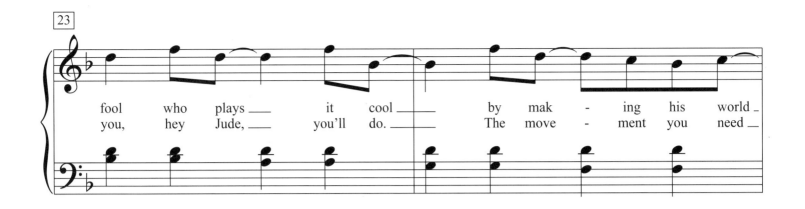

fool who plays ___ it cool ___ by mak - ing his world _
you, hey Jude, ___ you'll do. ___ The move - ment you need __

___ a lit - tle cold - er. ___ Da da da da ___ da da da da
___ is on ___ your shoul - der. ___ Da da da da ___ da da da da

da.
da.

1.

Hey ___

mp

2.

Hey
p

Jude, _____ don't make it bad; take a sad song ___ and make it

The Medallion Calls

from Walt Disney Pictures' PIRATES OF THE CARIBBEAN: THE CURSE OF THE BLACK PEARL

Music by Klaus Badelt
Arranged by Mona Rejino

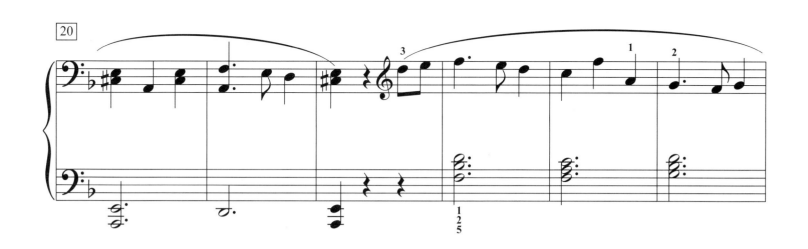

Satin Doll
from SOPHISTICATED LADIES

Words by Johnny Mercer
and Billy Strayhorn
Music by Duke Ellington
Arranged by Phillip Keveren

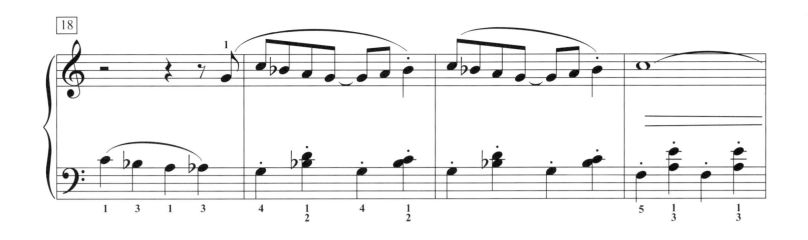

Star Wars
(Main Theme)
from STAR WARS, THE EMPIRE STRIKES BACK and RETURN OF THE JEDI

Music by John Williams
Arranged by Phillip Keveren

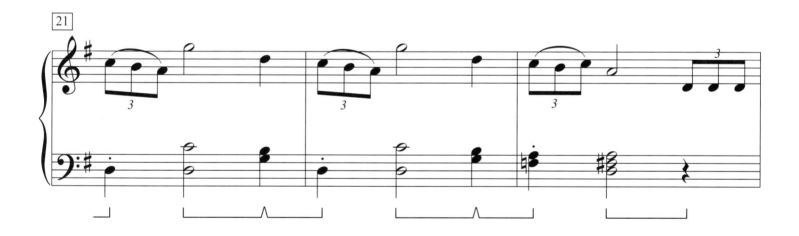

Sweet Caroline

Words and Music by
Neil Diamond
Arranged by Fred Kern

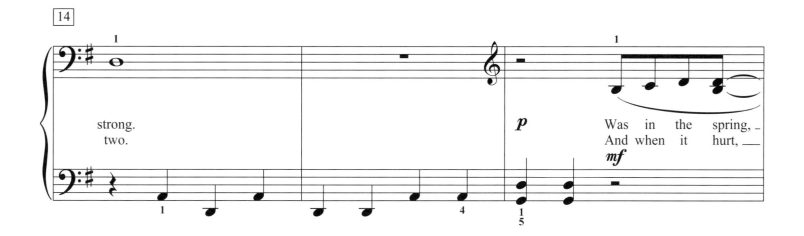

strong.
two.

p

mf

Was in the spring, —
And when it hurt, —

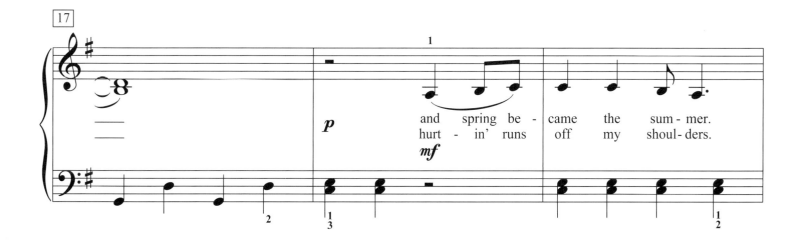

p

and spring be - came the sum - mer.
hurt - in' runs off my shoul - ders.

mf

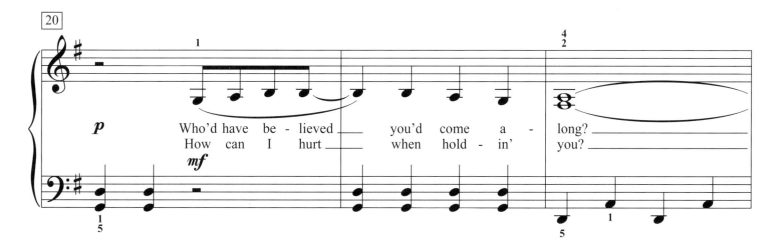

p

Who'd have be - lieved ___ you'd come a - long? ___
How can I hurt ___ when hold - in' you? ___

mf

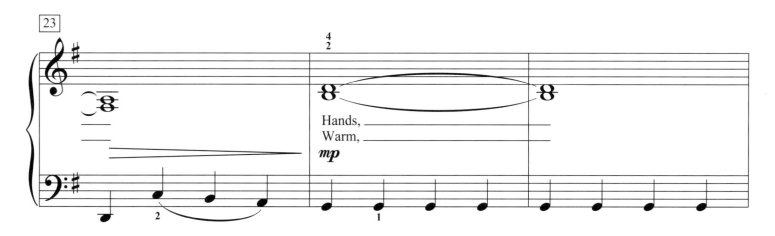

Hands, ___
Warm, ___

mp

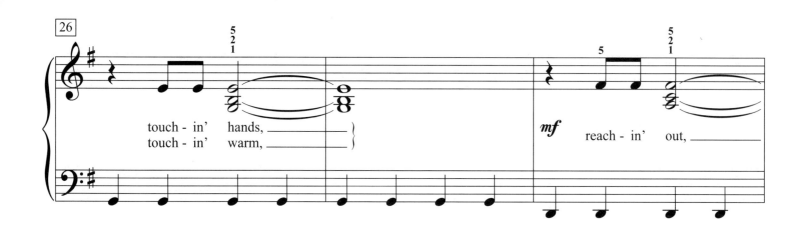

touch - in' hands, _____
touch - in' warm, _____

mf reach - in' out, _____

_____

touch - ing me, _____ touch - ing

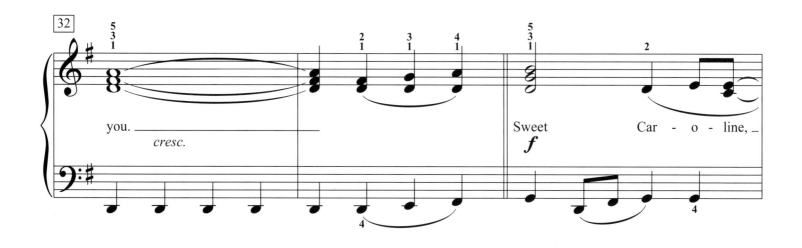

you. _____
cresc.

Sweet Car - o - line, _
f

_____
p

good times nev - er seemed so
f

good. _____ I've been in - clined _____

_____ to be - lieve _____ they nev - er

1. would, but now I... 2. would. _____

_____ Sweet Car - o - line. _____

Under the Sea

from Walt Disney's THE LITTLE MERMAID

Music by Alan Menken
Lyrics by Howard Ashman
Arranged by Fred Kern

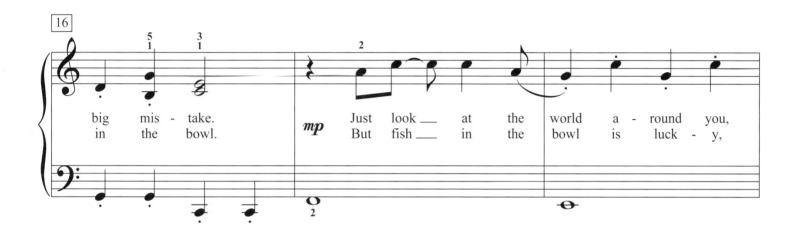

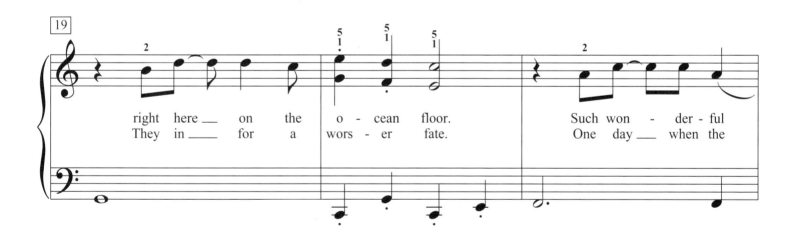

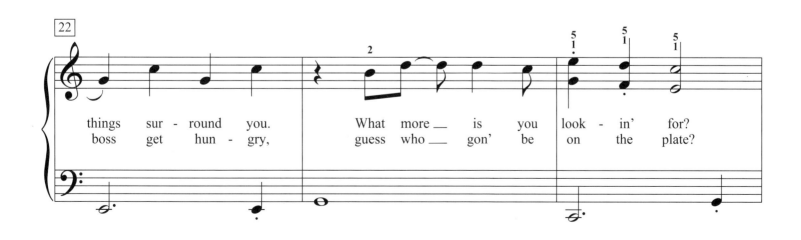

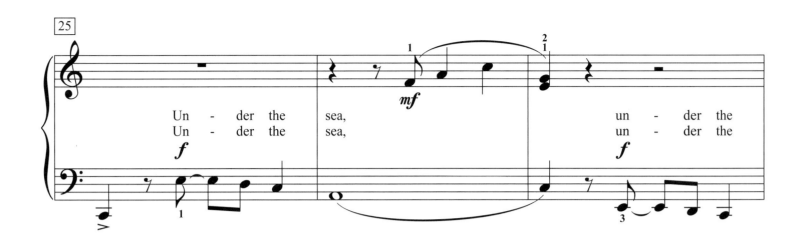

Under the sea, under the
Under the sea, under the

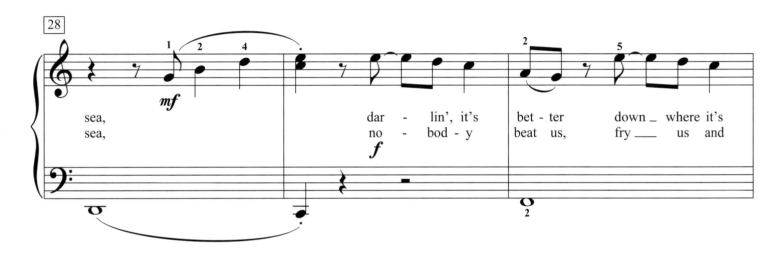

sea, dar - lin', it's bet - ter down __ where it's
sea, no - bod - y beat us, fry __ us and

wet - ter, take __ it from me. Up __ on the
eat us in __ fri - ca - see. We __ what the

shore they work __ all day. Out __ in the sun they slave __ a - way,
land folks love __ to cook, un - der the sea we off __ the hook.

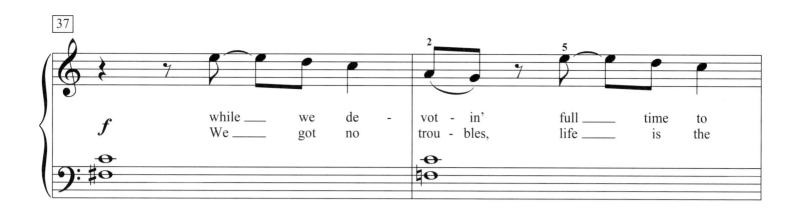

while ___ we de - vot - in' full ___ time to
We ___ got no trou - bles, life ___ is the

float - in' un - der the sea. *mf*
bub - bles un - der the

sea.

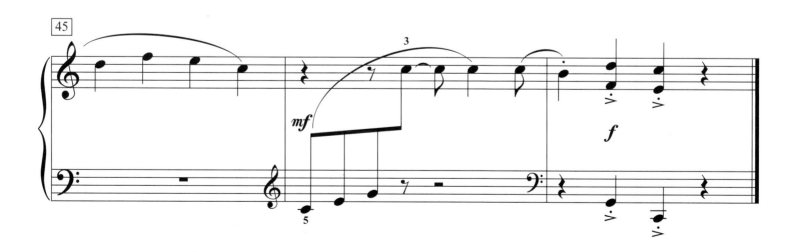

Georgia on My Mind

Words by Stuart Gorrell
Music by Hoagy Carmichael
Arranged by Phillip Keveren

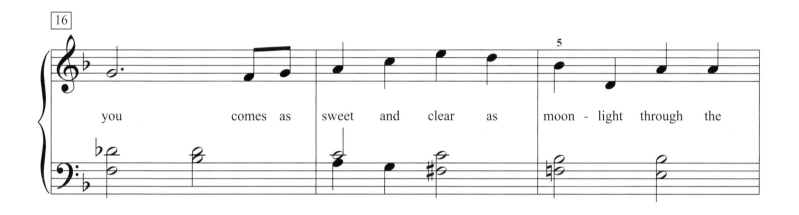

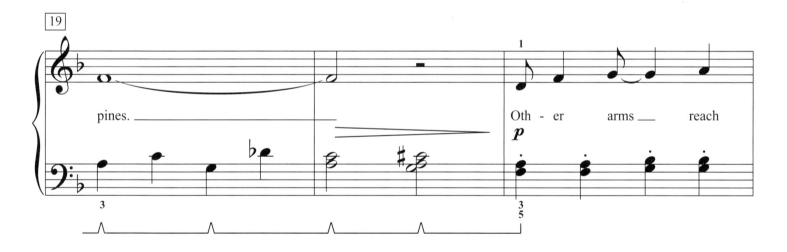

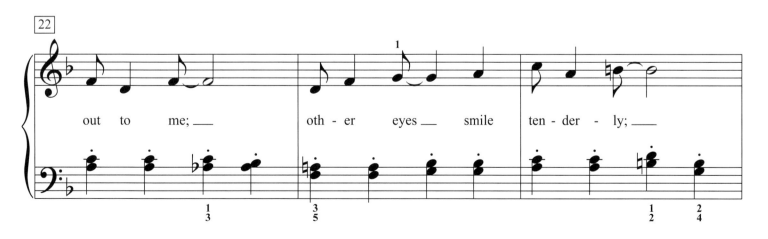

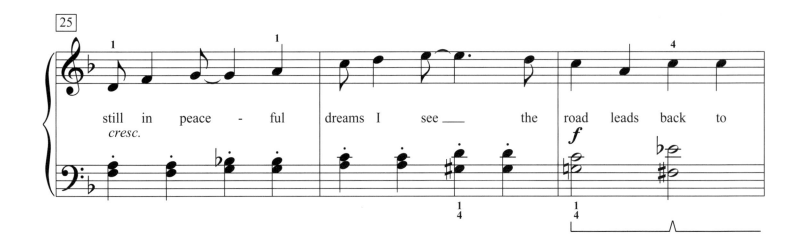

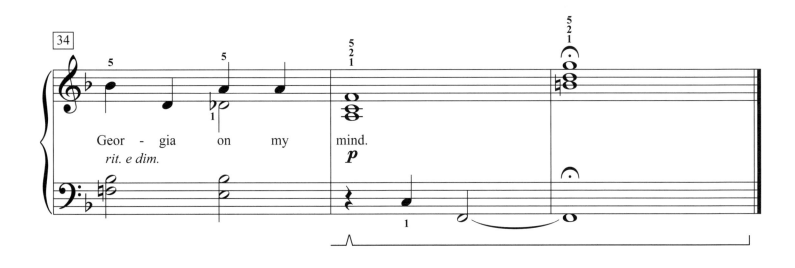